THE HAPPINESS LAB

FACILITATOR'S NOTES

A six-week experiment that
ſtimulates a conversation
about happiness

Paul Griffiths & Sharon Lanfear

Ugly Duckling Publishing
Oak House
Aylburton Business Centre
Stockwell Lane
Aylburton
Gloucestershire
GL15 6ST

CONTENTS

COPYRIGHT

Published by Ugly Duckling Publishing
Oak House
Aylburton Business Centre
Stockwell Lane
Aylburton
Gloucestershire
GL15 6ST
Email: office@theuglyducklingcompany.com
www.thehappinesslab.org

First edition 2016
Printed and bound in the UK

ISBN: 978-0-9935922-4-9

Acknowledgments
Miranda Lever (Editor), Sarah Kocher (Assistant Editor) and
Paul Worthy (Designer).

REGISTERING YOUR COURSE

We would like to journey with those who use The Happiness Lab material and, if you wish, advertise your course on The Happiness Lab website.

We are keen to support you in any way we can as you use The Happiness Lab material and, where possible, to help you share your experiences to encourage and inform others.

It costs nothing to register, and your information will not be passed on to anyone else.

ADDITIONAL BENEFITS FOR THOSE WHO REGISTER

- Additional information about Happiness Lab materials

- Notice of training days

- A newsletter with stories from those who are currently running the course, plus helpful hints and tips

- Discounts on Happiness Lab materials and training courses

- Your courses listed on The Happiness Lab website

HOW TO REGISTER

Please send details of your course, the location, dates and the contact name to office@thehappinesslab.org, or write to:

The Ugly Duckling Company
PO Box 31
Lydney
GL15 6YP

FEEDBACK

LEADER'S FEEDBACK

We want your feedback. We want to celebrate with you the stories of where the course has gone well and how people have been equipped to flourish that little bit more. It is also important to us to know where it didn't work or what we could have done differently or better so as to make your experience as course leader and the delegate's experience more meaningful.

We are interested in finding out:

- How suitable the material was for you and for the delegates
- What you thought of the quality of the materials
- Where you ran the course
- What numbers were involved
- What you wish you had known before you ran the course
- How we could help you to run the course better

FEEDBACK FROM PARTICIPANTS

We have created an online survey to obtain feedback from those who attend The Happiness Lab.

Please encourage all delegates to access the survey at the end of the course.

As part of the survey, we are inviting delegates to join a group of people who will engage with us over the next 10 years exploring what makes people happy.

HOW TO OFFER FEEDBACK

To give feedback please go to www.thehappinesslab.org and click on the feedback button.

GRAPHIC DESIGN

WE'RE HERE TO HELP

One of the services offered by The Ugly Duckling Company is graphic design. If in running THL you require assistance in preparing your marketing materials, then we are more than happy to help. We can add your details to all of the materials you require for £10 or equivalent currency.

The
INTRODUCTION

WHAT IS THE HAPPINESS LAB?

The Happiness Lab is a six-week experimental course. The course creates space for delegates to explore what psychologists, doctors, faith leaders and other delegates on the course have to say about happiness.

Rather than offering a theoretical explanation of how we can increase our happiness level, the programme combines the presentation of what experts have to say on the topic and an opportunity to try out what they are saying. Following each week's session those on the course are encouraged to try several happiness exercises.

Through six independent but connected experiments, delegates are given an opportunity to explore and test how gratitude and savouring, practising acts of kindness, learning to forgive, investing in friends and family, taking care of your body and soul, and developing coping strategies could make us happier people.

With the narrative that to be human is to be spiritual, THL experiments with the mantra that happiness comes from living well and that you live well when you live as a spiritual person in a material age. In each session, as part of opening up the subject for exploration, we contemplate the spiritual dimension—if indeed there is one—of that week's disciplines.

This resource does not offer a prescriptive answer. Yes, professionals have pointed to indicators that could aid someone's journey to their earthly "nirvana", but the purpose of the course is to help delegates conduct their own experiments and come to their own conclusions.

The reason for exploring this topic alongside others is that it might just be a little bit more fun—like going to the gym with friends as opposed to going on your own.

With regard to what outcomes those on the course and those hosting the course should be working for (or looking for), in our opinion it is that people are better equipped to flourish as they navigate their way through life.

On a practical level, the goals for the course could be that individuals:

- have several new exercises that they have implemented into their daily life
- have access to exercises that will help them live at a higher happiness level
- have an understanding of the discussion around each of the key disciplines identified as leading to a happier life
- are noticeably happier at the end of the six weeks!

WHAT'S IN THE STARTER PACK?

The starter pack contains the materials outlined below. These have been put together to enable you to run the course and give the delegates who attend the best experience we can offer.

FACILITATOR'S NOTES

The Facilitator's Notes contain information about running the course. They enable you to explore topics worth thinking about before you start and give advice about running discussion groups. There are also suggestions for the content for each session.

DELEGATE'S GUIDE - 10 COPIES

Covering each of the themes in the course, every chapter contains an opportunity to reflect on the topic aided by the insights of a variety of professionals; the story of those who have already attended the course; an opportunity to journal; questions to reflect on; and happiness exercises to try. Each starter pack contains ten delegate workbooks.

See tips to offer delegates about using their workbook in Session 1.

DVD

The DVD contains the following:

•   a one-minute promo video

•   a ten-minute taster video that sets up the course content which would be ideal to play at a launch event or at an evening where people can find out more about THL

•   6 x 25 minute episodes, each relating to the six sessions of the course.

MEDIA PACK

The media pack, which can be downloaded from THL website, contains:

- postcard invites
- posters
- flyers
- a PVC banner template
- web banners
- data slides
- other templates that you may find helpful in letting people know about this course.

All the files are editable. (Do let us know if you have any problems accessing these files or need help with graphic design.)

101 HAPPINESS EXPERIMENTS

THL is not just a place to think about what makes us happier; it also helps us experiment with different exercises that we can build into our lives. As a starter, we offer the resource *101 Happiness Experiments*. Most of the ideas in this book can be built into our daily lives.

More copies can be obtained from THL web shop.

THE 8 SECRETS OF HAPPINESS X 1

Written by Paul Griffiths and Martin Robinson, *The 8 Secrets of Happiness* explores what psychologists, doctors and faith leaders have to say about happiness.

With a mantra that happiness comes from living well and you live well when you realise that you are a spiritual person in a material age, the book engages with the insights of professionals and the spiritual dynamics of what they have to say.

To help facilitators prepare for the course, we have included *The 8 Secrets of Happiness* book and would encourage you to read it.

In reading through the Delegate's Guide you will notice that we also encourage those participating on the course to read the book.

More copies can be obtained from THL web shop.

Find space during a tough day.

Taken from *101 Happiness Experiments*

COURSE CONTENT

Launch Event (optional): Happiness is...? (This can also be used during the first session if you decide not to do a launch event.)

Designed to run over six weeks, THL explores the following themes:

- Session 1: Focussing on Gratitude and Savouring
  Learn the art of savouring—what it is; what its effects are; and how to begin to count our blessings by saying "thank you".

- Session 2: Practising Acts of Kindness
  Understand what kindness looks like; think more deeply about how it is offered and received; and plan some acts of kindness.

- Session 3: Learning to Forgive
  Define forgiveness and its boundaries; understand some of the skills needed to develop forgiveness; and to begin to think about how to put it into practice personally.

- Session 4: Investing in Friends and Family
  Understand and act on the fundamental importance of relationships; what makes for good relationships; and what might prevent them?

- Session 5: Looking after your Body and Soul
  How to understand ourselves as "whole beings" (body, mind, soul, spirit); describe the influences upon us; and to encourage each of us to take responsibility for our body and soul.

- Session 6: Developing Coping Strategies
  To explore coping strategies for when life is difficult; to identify what options are available; and to consider which ones we already employ when life is difficult.

AMBIENCE

We want people to enjoy coming on THL and to enjoy it so much that they want to bring their friends along next time!

This course is about creating an environment where people feel safe: a place where they feel they can contribute without being judged; question without being corrected; and listen and speak without being interrupted.

We want each guest to feel respected and honoured in our company.

The list of qualities that we want to encourage as part of the course includes:

WELCOMING

Mother Teresa observed that the greatest epidemic in the world was not leprosy or cancer, but loneliness. Do make a very real effort to welcome people to the group every week, both formally and informally. Look out for those who have chosen to attend the group on their own. If at all possible, when selecting people to help you run the course, choose individuals who are engaging and who take a keen interest in the lives of others.

WARMTH

Friendliness is more than being welcoming. It is about being interested in the person, remembering what they say from week to week, and being genuinely pleased to see them.

FUN

We are not suggesting that you tell a couple of jokes every session or try to be a stand-up comedian if you are presenting the material, or that you play pranks on people. Rather, you should take time over the six weeks to laugh and smile at those moments when it is appropriate and right to do so.

HONESTY

There has to be a caution associated with the notion of being an "honest person". There are occasions when it would be inappropriate and unwise to open yourself up and tell strangers your deepest and darkest secrets. That said, there is a place for acknowledging that you have had struggles during the course of your life, that you don't know the answer to every question you are asked, and that you are still on a personal journey of discovery yourself.

LISTENING

For many, listening is a lost art. Sometimes during a conversation people are quiet, not because they are actively listening to the words being spoken by the person they are with, but because they are waiting for the first moment of silence so that they can jump in with what they want to say. One of the ways in which we greatly honour other people is by learning to genuinely listen to them when they speak.

GRACE

Our understanding of being gracious is being someone who does all they can to cheer the other person on. It is about not putting yourself, your needs and your hang-ups in the way of serving the other person.

CHALLENGE

As the weeks go by, things may be said that you disagree with strongly. It is OK to disagree, as long as it's done in a gracious, humble way. It is also OK to challenge people to really think about what they say or believe–again, as long as this is done in a gracious and humble way.

OPENNESS

There are no taboos on subject matter or on opinion.

CONCLUSION

No Happiness Lab leader should assume that all of these qualities are present each session. Therefore, we would encourage you to engage with your helpers in understanding and committing yourselves to being the best you can be for the good of others.

USING THE FACILITATOR'S NOTES

The authors are from a generation where you expect people to read the instruction manual before switching the device on! The implications of not doing so is that the device appears to be broken or isn't used properly.

We have written this guide because we think it would be helpful for those running the course to create some space to think about what they are embarking on. No leader's guide is ever going to cover all the bases and there is an argument for simply getting on with it and seeing how it goes. These notes could be helpful if the course does not work or you encounter difficulties.

That said, the pages of this book open up conversation about what THL is: how to create the right environment; how to invite people; how to lead discussion groups; and also some thoughtful pieces on subjects such as spiritual anthropology.

It would be well worth lending the book to those who might lead the course with you or be involved in facilitating discussion groups so that they could benefit from its contents.

You don't need to read the whole book, but it might be helpful to dip in and out as the course proceeds.

DELEGATES FIRST

One of the temptations in facilitating THL is to spend your time making sure that everyone on your team is doing all that they should be doing. It is important to encourage your team and manage them through their tasks; however, as the host you have a primary duty to be free to engage with your guests as they arrive and during the time that they are present at the session.

Remember that the discussions and the members that participate in them are from different backgrounds, with different life experiences and different understandings of how the world works. In order to create a space that all participants feel comfortable in, a facilitator needs not only to welcome others' viewpoints into the conversation, but also to be willing to speak when shared vulnerability can put others at ease.

Several of The Happiness Lab sessions touch on what it means to be in relationship with others and how those relationships affect us. Maintaining appropriate contact with your group members can help them to feel encouraged, included, and more invested in the course.

Demonstrate the principles of what it means to be a generally good human. This can be a helpful exercise for all of us to live and work more positively in community with others.

FACILITATOR

Humans form relationship based on a desire for honest connection. As a facilitator, you can help foster this connection by committing to be your most authentic self, and asking others to do the same.

Where appropriate and possible, take time to find out how people are generally. If there is an opportunity (perhaps during the meal or over refreshments), then do talk to them about how they are finding the course.

Plan A will not always be what reaches or engages your audience. Some of the biggest breakthroughs come when a facilitator is willing to adapt and let the session take a shape that best speaks to those participating in it. This can be spur of the moment or planned if you realize partway through the course that your group's needs could be met in a different way.

The
KNOWLEDGE

HAPPINESS

Is it possible to be deeply happy: to have a depth of happiness that sparkles in the routine of everyday life and which overflows even in life's most difficult circumstances and darkest moments?

In *The Road Less Travelled*, bestselling author M. Scott Peck focuses on his conviction concerning one of the greatest truths about life. He faces us with the core reality that life is difficult. He then goes on to argue that many people attempt to avoid this reality. Others, though, do want to know whether there is a quality of happiness that we can access as we face up to, live in and live with the realities of life—a happiness ride that lasts longer than the occasional four minutes on a rollercoaster.

Historians tell us that humankind has always searched for happiness. Plato studied the good life in his academy and Aristotle set up his own college to look at what human flourishing would mean. Over time, Buddha, Confucius, Patanjali, and Jesus have all added their insights about this insatiable drive.

Today, this search for the "blessed life" is expressed in the 56 million hits that the Internet search engine, Google, gets for the word "happiness", or the fact that there are over 60,000 books in print whose titles are connected with the theme of this earthly nirvana. Recently, *Time* magazine dedicated a special edition to the subject

of happiness. It brought together a significant array of research on the subject, most of which was instigated as a consequence of a challenge issued to the American Psychological Association by their incoming president in 1998. In his presidential speech he noted that throughout its history, psychology had been preoccupied with the idea of making people less miserable (taking them from –5 to 0, as he puts it). He proposed that psychology should actually change its emphasis towards a quest for happiness (taking people from 0 to +5).

From this challenge flowed a large number of studies that all approached different dimensions of the question of happiness. *Time* magazine brought these various studies together and summarised their findings. They wanted to explore and answer the basic question, "What is it that makes people happy?"

It appears that very few people today report that they are happy. An opinion poll by GfK NOP identified that only 36 per cent of the UK population consider themselves to be very happy. Interestingly, along with those conducted in the USA, this poll identified a downward trend in the nations' happiness. Believe it or not, we describe ourselves as more miserable than our parents did at an equivalent time in their lives.

So why is the pursuit of happiness so central to our concerns? Why do we feel that our lives are miserable? And how do we understand the happiness that we seek?

WHAT IS HAPPINESS?

When it comes to defining happiness, most people are at a loss for words. A major reason for this is that the concept is so difficult to pin down. Money and material possessions are often associated with the attainment of happiness, but describing what happiness would look and feel like is much more tough.

Our western concept of happiness can be traced back to the Greek word eudaimonia, which consists of the words eu, which means "good" or "well-being", and daimon, meaning "spirit" or "one's lot in life". The problem comes when we attempt to flesh out what that may mean in our modern daily lives.

If nothing else, such ambiguity, as philosopher Henri Bergson commented, means that "each individual may interpret it in their own way". The capacity for personal choice is highly valued in our individual and multi-optioned society. So happiness can be as varied as a holiday, a new car, or doing better than you thought you would in your annual work appraisal. It is something that is pleasing, involves the emotions and can be understood as a passing or momentary experience. In fact, our English word "happy" derives from the middle English word hap, which relates to the idea of happenstance or good fortune.

Many studies have emanated from a range of different disciplines, and thus more formal definitions of happiness have been attempted. However, because of the complexity of the subject, it quickly becomes obvious that no common agreement exists.

In the laboratory of biology, happiness can be defined as that which occurs when a human being connects with the brain's pleasure centre. By contrast, in the debating chamber of politics, politicians are aware that what keeps voters happy is the feeling that the economy is doing well so that people feel prosperous and confident about their future prospects.

While on the couch of psychology, happiness may be associated with teaching people to see the glass half-full as opposed to half-empty. At the popular level, it is about "learned optimism". You can only be as happy as you decide to be. This is quite different from what is seen in the estate agent's window where happiness is advertised as the possibility of buying a house in the Forest of Dean area (in a recent poll the Forest of Dean was voted one of the happiest places to live in the UK).

Advertisers would have us believe that designer label consumption or commitment to particular brands will bring happiness to our lives. The list of definitions becomes almost endless as we think about the various perspectives offered by employers, friends, family or even those who may want to offer counselling of various kinds.

Clearly these are particular or partial views of happiness. A more substantial view of the nature of happiness can be accessed by considering what we may call the wisdom of the ages in relation to happiness. The eastern tradition, for example, says that all of us are filled with inappropriate desires and that as we rid ourselves of these, so we begin to discover happiness. Thus, according to this tradition, our failure to obtain happiness does not relate to our absence of material possessions but to our desire to have them in the first place.

Then there is the tradition explored by mystics in both the East and West—the ecstatic tradition. This tradition explores how it is in union with a divine being that we find happiness. Life, then, should be a continual search for transcendent experiences.

Since the nineteenth century, the western tradition—which has generally placed more value on the material world—has tended to suggest that precisely because we are material beings, happiness lies not in spiritual experiences of one kind or another, but in the very practical and attainable areas of health and wealth.

A more recent refinement of that "health and wealth" tradition recognises that we do have other needs and it has developed a range of self-realization theories which suggests that true happiness is found in discovering one's true self and destiny. That does not necessarily mean an obsession with oneself; it could possibly mean getting involved in a cause of some kind—a cause greater than oneself. There are many people today who, for example, find meaning in speaking up for the marginalised in our society or campaigning for a better environment.

So, is there some way we can navigate these various views of East and West, of ancient and modern? We can find a clue to such an approach as we look at an older western tradition that comes to us from the ancient world of both the Greeks and Christian mystics and thinkers. This older tradition brings balance by claiming that we are spiritual beings living in a material world. The spiritual is affirmed but the physical is not rejected—it too has a part to play. The suggestion is that when both come together in appropriate ways, we can discover the happy life. It is not just about focusing on the spiritual side of who we are, nor about focusing purely on the physical side of our makeup, but rather by combining both in healthy ways that we are enabled to discover the kind of life that is deeply fulfilling.

In such an approach, dancing with happiness is more a consequence than a purpose. It is more a perpetual state than a momentary emotion. It is more about how you live than what you have. And it is more about what is happening on the inside than how we present ourselves at the superficial level, because happiness includes our emotions: it involves our intellect or mind; it connects to particular activities; but it also intersects with the spiritual. Happiness is therefore not the goal so much as the outcome of particular ways of living. These ways of living enable us to connect the physical with the spiritual in creative, life-enhancing ways.

WHAT MAKES PEOPLE HAPPY?

Some time ago in the UK, the BBC ran a series of features on the science of happiness in which they asked the question "Is there a formula for happiness?" It doesn't take long when scanning the book titles in the "Mind, Body and Soul" section of any good bookstore to discover that there is a wide variety of proposed formulas for happiness. Out there in the marketplace where one size does not fit all, there seems to be hundreds of formulas for happiness, some of which seem very superficial and are certainly untested. Happy to experiment with their own formula, some individuals have a selection box for happiness that can sometimes be shocking and a little too physical for others. In the business of happiness, there is sometimes a difference between imagined longings and researched reality.

The question has been asked for millennia, with the ancient Greeks offering many schools of thought. Socrates advocated self-knowledge as the path to happiness. Plato's 'The Allegory of the Cave' influenced many western thinkers to believe that happiness is found by taking scholarly advice. Aristotle believed that happiness is constituted by moderate, rational activity in accordance with virtue over taking scholarly advice. The Epicureans believed in reaching happiness through the enjoyment of simple pleasures. The Stoics meanwhile believed they could remain happy by being objective and reasonable.

CIRCUMSTANCES

For those who equate happiness with the presence of favourable circumstances, their shopping list consists of items that aid personal fulfilment. Therefore, happiness is to do with how our career is going, the depth of our relationships, the state of our health, the intensity and frequency of our sex life, or the quality of the food we eat. It is about our lifestyle and all of the parts that make it so. A fairly universal finding from research suggests that beyond a certain point, there is almost no relationship between money (or material possessions) and happiness and yet, when interviewed, most people living in the western world strongly associate money with happiness. However, as UK economist Richard Layard states, the relationship between our perceived wealth and our perceived happiness is complex. For example, richer nations do not report any greater degree of happiness than poorer nations. When whole societies become wealthier, the degree of happiness reported by the

poorest groups and by the wealthiest groups in that society does not change. The only significant reported shift in happiness ratios is accompanied by a perception of a greater fairness or equality in society. Such a shift is connected to values, ethics and spirituality.

For others—for those who have accomplished many of their personal goals—there comes the surprising discovery that such an achievement does not necessarily lead to the happiness they seek. The tennis player John McEnroe tells the story of how, having reached the pinnacle of his sporting career, he did not feel that it led to the contentment and happiness that he had anticipated. For McEnroe and for others, the quality of relationships that they enjoyed became much more important.

BACK TO NATURE

Since the 1960s there has been a renewed regard for the environment and a more positive evaluation of nature. Some people have wanted to live simpler lives that are more in tune with nature. One example of this is that of the many hundreds of people from all over the world who have spent time living at the Findhorn community in north-east Scotland. It is here that they have attempted to reconnect with nature in terms of both healing and happiness.

POSITIVE PSYCHOLOGY

As we have mentioned, the recent rise of interest in happiness seems to flow from a challenge thrown out to psychologists to take the issue of happiness more seriously. The results have been fascinating in that popular perceptions of what brings happiness (for example, material wealth) cannot be substantiated by hard research. Actual research suggests that the softer issues, relating more to the spiritual dimension of life, turn out to be at least as important if not more important than the material factors.

SPIRITUALITY

Knowing how to connect the material with the spiritual is a crucial element in the happiness stakes. Yet a review of web pages dealing with happiness reveals that few, if any, mention those vital spiritual factors. The BBC, in an attempt to kick-start the debate on what should be in our happiness formula, mentioned the need for personal meaning and within that implied the necessity of connecting with something outside of oneself. Oliver James, a

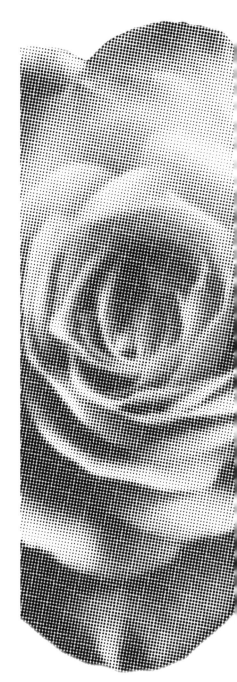

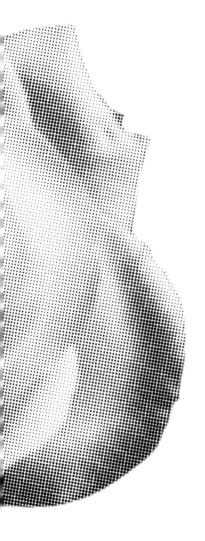

British psychologist, points out that religious people are much less likely to have what he calls "virus goals or motivations". He connects the capacity to live without affluenza (the bloated, sluggish, unfulfilled feeling that pervades twenty-first century life) and the happiness it brings with deeper spiritual values.

HOW DOES THE SPIRITUAL RELATE TO BEING HAPPY?

For an increasing minority, there is a growing awareness that happiness and spiritual discovery are deeply connected. So how may we approach happiness from the perspective of spirituality? Just as importantly, what do we mean by spirituality in such a context?

In recent times, those who have an interest in the health of the workplace have been drawn to the relevance of spirituality. This is reflected in the science of management theory, where there is enormous growth in the study of spirituality in the workplace.

In today's world, business gurus and trainers talk about a manager's SQ, which refers to their spiritual intelligence quotient. This is something that, when combined with EQ (emotional intelligence) and IQ, has the potential to create great leaders. This is because in becoming more aware of who they are and what makes them tick, these influencers are able to focus on developing deeper and more significant aspects of their being.

As we have already suggested, the spiritual dimension to life is embedded in the Greek word for happiness and the aim of this course is to look at the connection between spirituality and happiness. THL is not merely about creating some light relief during a tough afternoon at work–welcome as that may be–but rather is concerned to develop the presence of happiness that helps to put long-term joy into life and also builds sufficient resilience that we may better face up to life's hardest journeys. To recall the words of the writer M. Scott Peck, life is difficult, but those difficulties can be overcome in rewarding ways.

In drawing our understanding of who we are from an older western tradition that recognizes us as spiritual people in a material world, we are going to look at how the spiritual dimension to life, when connected with our daily living, provides a source for deeper happiness. In other words, how do we connect the "me" that we feel ourselves to be—which is more than just the sum total of our physical attributes—with the physicality of our daily life?

The spiritual dimension that people are increasingly becoming aware of is suggested in the discovery that seven out of ten people in the UK pray on a regular basis. Surprisingly, research reports that one of the most frequently asked questions on the part of those outside of any formal religious structures is "What is the spiritual realm and how does it impact my life?"

IS IT STILL POSSIBLE TO BE HAPPY WHEN LIFE IS DIFFICULT?

Happiness is not dependent on favourable outward circumstances alone. For many people today, life is difficult—not all of the time but certainly for some of it. We may not see our lives as obvious material for the writing of a tragedy, but most of us have experienced sadness of some kind. The deeper happiness that this book seeks to describe does not remove all sadness, but rather emphasises that deeper happiness can be found in those who outwardly do not have many reasons to smile.

AND SO TO THE SESSIONS...

The search for happiness runs deep in contemporary society. Many magazines run articles on happiness and ageing, happiness and your weight, happiness and your heart, even happiness and your kitchen. For many people it has become the Holy Grail—the cup that offers us quality, if not eternal, life. So how do we make sense of so much material? How do we chart a course that can give us some practical direction in the midst of so much data?

Our intention in the following chapters is to help you and your delegates answer these questions. In order to do so, we shall unpack the findings of the research conducted by writers and thinkers and then published, as aforementioned, by *Time* magazine. The findings are summarised under six major headings. We will take you through each of these and reveal the golden thread that runs through them all—that there is a spiritual side of humanity which cannot be overlooked in the pursuit of happiness.

First published by Lion Hudson in *The 8 Secrets of Happiness* by Paul Griffiths and Martin Robinson.

SPIRITUAL ANTHROPOLOGY

In his book *Something There*, anthropologist David Hay states that ten out of ten people in the UK have had some form of spiritual experience.

On first reading it is understandable why some people struggle to agree with Hay's findings. It was not too long ago that some were declaring that "God [is] dead". Additionally, many prominent celebrities and academics are keen to promote atheism.

It should be noted that an adherence to the existence of God, or the denial of God, is not our definition of spiritual. For us, to be human is to be spiritual. It is the belief and life practice (whether consciously or subconsciously) that there is more to life than we can see, touch, or reason. It is the belief that there is something beyond us which interacts with who we are and the world about us.

ANECDOTAL EVIDENCE THAT WE ARE SPIRITUAL BEINGS

Despite the vocal declaration of some that acknowledgment of the spiritual is nothing more than a denial of our DNA, a quick observation of what is going on around us indicates that there is considerable evidence to support Hay's worldview.

For instance, large supermarkets sell spiritual magazines. Why? There is no doubt that these stores have an evangelistic agenda, which is to win the world for their brand. As a business, they sell products for one reason and one reason alone: because people buy them. So, why would an individual buy a spiritual magazine? Surely such magazines are bought because people want to read them.

Further evidence that we are spiritual beings can be seen in the way that in most high-street bookshops there is now a genre of authorship called "spiritual writers". Added to this is the running of many "body, mind and soul" festivals; the number of films that carry a spiritual storyline; and the fact that seven out of ten people in the UK claim to pray.

One last piece of anecdotal evidence comes from the world of business. There are said to be six management styles and for many years it was believed that a person's capacity to lead others was dependent on their IQ (Intellectual Quotient). Following a book by Daniel Goldman which explored the influence of our emotional life on the way that we lead, many leadership coaches now recognise that our capacity to lead others is based on our IQ and our EQ. Over the last twenty years, considerable thought has been given to the role of a spiritual capacity in the leadership of others. Although not yet mainstream, there is an acknowledgment among some that the ability of a person to lead others is actually a combination of their IQ, EQ, and SQ.

THE TYPE OF SPIRITUAL EXPERIENCES THAT PEOPLE HAVE

It might be helpful to consider the evidence that Hay collected that led him to believe that to be human is to be spiritual. He identified seven experiences that those interviewed displayed. These are:

- a pattern to some of life's events

- God's presence

- unnamed but divine presence

- answered prayer

- a sacred presence in nature

- the presence of the dead

- the presence of evil.

Hay notes that not everyone could recall spiritual experiences or readily accredit these experiences to a spiritual reality. However, with some help, they were able to join the dots for themselves and make appropriate tags.

UNCERTAINTY WITH THE SPIRITUAL

In citing all of the above—that we are spiritual people living in the material world and that with some help individuals are able to identify experiences that can be connected with the spiritual—it is important to note that many people are unsure of what it means to

be spiritual, what the spiritual world is, and how it interacts with the world about them. Research conducted by Coventry Cathedral on the questions asked by those who are outside of the church but who are interested in spirituality noted that a big question for many is, "What is the spiritual realm and how does it impact my life?"

COMMUNICATION

Hopefully delegates on THL are on the course because they want to find out more about happiness. The goal of the course leader or facilitator is to create the best learning environment for each of the delegates.

The material in this section addresses the communication event and learning styles.

In preparation for hosting THL it is advisable to think through your communication skill set and consider how you can best facilitate the learning of those you will be leading through THL. As part of your preparation, do talk to those from a teaching profession if possible.

Three simple questions to ask the group at the end of each session, which offers them a moment of reflection and you an opportunity for feedback, are:

> What did I enjoy?
> What have I learned?
> What will I take away with me?

THE COMMUNICATION EVENT

Communication is purposeful, involves a process, is multidimensional, and requires skills that can be learned. It is both straightforward ("Please can you pass me the salt?") and highly complex ("Do you think I am like my mother?").

The goal of communication is to share, to make common. It is about an exchange of thought, feeling, meaning, or information between two or more people.

Aspects of good communication include the reading of someone's body language, listening to what is being said (or not said), and reflecting back to someone what they are communicating. It involves the use of questions and appropriate language.

THE COMMUNICATION EVENT

When it comes to understanding the communication event there are numerous ways that it can be illustrated. In running THL it is important that we have a grasp of what is involved.

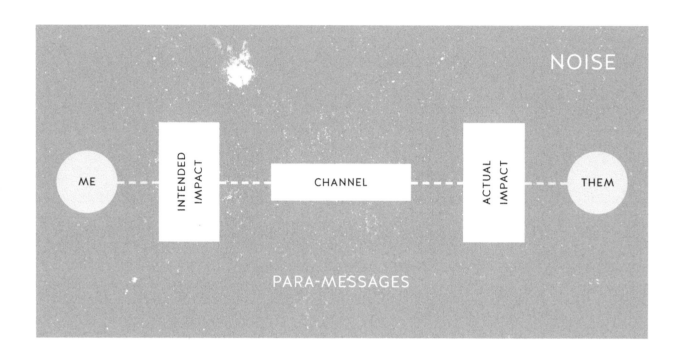

Me – When we come to any communication experience, we come to it bringing a lifetime of experiences, particular fears, and prejudices. As a child, a friend of ours was mocked by his parents every time he offered an opinion about something going on in the world. Today, whenever he offers an opinion on world affairs, he always does so in an unsure and fearful way, wary of how he will be treated.

Intended impact — When we enter the communication event we do so with a goal and an intended impact that we hope to make on the person that we are relating to. It is important that we think through, as best we can, what it is that we want to say and consider how it will affect the people we are going to be speaking to. Someone once said that "simplicity rests on the other side of complexity". The better we understand what it is that we want to say, the simpler and more effective we will be in its communication.

The channel or medium through which we communicate — There are many ways that we can communicate with one another, and each of them presents us with challenges and advantages. If we are going to speak with a person, then this will include voice, facial expressions, and general body language. Depending on where this will happen will mean that we have to think through the ambience of the room, the seating arrangements, and the decor and comfort of those present. What is important is that we choose the best medium for what we want to communicate.

Actual impact — This is the effect of our message on the person that we are communicating with. What will not come as a surprise to an experienced communicator is that what we say is very often not what is heard. We also need to note that saying something once, even if it is said with great clarity, offers no guarantee that the person has heard us.

Them — Those that we communicate with are not blank slates. People come to the communication process with their own stories, experiences, and thoughts that have been built up over many years and the last 24 hours.

Noise — Here the word is used to mean more than auditory interference. "Noise" includes any interference in the context of the exchange. It will include environmental factors, such as visual and auditory stimuli, and also includes the mood, recent experiences, physical and mental state, and so on.

Para-messages – These are unintentional messages that run alongside your intended message. When speaking to a group of people recently, one of the authors of the course used several illustrations about their family to explain what he was trying to say. After the event he was approached by someone who wanted to thank him for speaking so well about the family. They had completely missed what he was trying to say and instead heard his remarks on the family.

Interaction – It is important that we appreciate that communication is a two-way process and as such can be started by others and, of course, includes responses from others.

CONCLUSION

Feedback is very important as it offers us the opportunity to assess how we are doing as communicators. As such, in running THL we would encourage everyone who is involved in presenting the material to be offered feedback on how they are coming across to the audience. In terms of how guests might be interacting with the material, an appropriate system of obtaining feedback would be useful. This is something that can be obtained through a small group leaders' debriefing session, or in simply asking people over an informal meal how they are finding the course.

HOW PEOPLE LEARN

We all learn in different ways. Technically described as learning styles, everyone has a natural orientation to the way that they take in information, work through it, understand and then remember it.

In developing THL our goal has been to connect with each of these learning styles. Admittedly, you have to think in shades of grey, as each session connects to different learning styles at different points. The challenge will be to encourage those whose learning style is not being employed to stay engaged and work through that phase of the programme.

There are four recognised learning styles. These are auditory, visual, kinaesthetic, and reading and writing.

AUDITORY

Listening and speaking are the key ways that those with an auditory learning style engage with information. They are the ones who will be asking the questions or wanting to think out loud during conversation.

KINAESTHETIC

Group exercises and the opportunity to practise what you have been speaking about during the session are key learning moments for kinaesthetic learners. These are individuals who learn best by being able to touch or do.

VISUAL

The delegate's workbook and an opportunity to watch the DVD for each session will be important in helping visual learners engage in the material. Think about how you can visually illustrate what you or others are saying.

READING AND WRITING

The opportunity to journal and take notes are key learning aids with this group. It would also be helpful for them to read *The 8 Secrets of Happiness* and to access the Delegate's Guide.

Used by other professionals, here is a simple summary to filter how you deliver the material as you host THL.

see it

hear/ say it

it

do it

ADULTS LEARN WHEN THEY WANT TO

As noted above, our belief is that those on the course are there because they want to learn. They might not know what it is that they want to learn and there is a possibility that some of the insights they obtain might not be the most welcome. Nevertheless, our goal is to aid everyone in their life-long learning.

Acknowledging that you do not know it all and that there is wisdom in the room to be gleaned from the delegates themselves, the purpose of each session is to frame a topic, offer some reflections and insights, encourage the delegates to explore these for themselves both individually and as a group, and then to have a go at trying out some practices for themselves.

Insights gained by the delegates thinking through an issue or talking to others on the course will be owned and integrated more deeply into their understanding as opposed to them being told what it is that they should think.

Self-learning and group discovery are important to facilitate ownership and practical application of ideas into an individual's life.

As the group facilitator, try to think more in terms of what people are learning rather than what you are teaching.

MARKETING

How to advertise your course

Every context will necessitate a different marketing strategy. Some of the contexts that the course will be run in (e.g. a gym) will provide some pre-existing marketing networks, and if you run the course at a local doctor's surgery then the hope would be that they will point patients in your direction. In some scenarios it will be up to you to devise your own marketing strategy to bring people together to attend the course. From our experience, the best way to fill up a course is through friends bringing their friends along, whatever the context. Word of mouth is the best form of marketing!

PUBLICITY MATERIALS

We have created a variety of advertising materials that you can use to promote your course. Examples of these can be seen at the end of these facilitator's notes. They include: postcard invites, posters, web banners, data slides, PVC banners, Facebook and Twitter banners, and promo and preview videos. If you have ideas about other tools that you think would be helpful, then do contact us at office@theuglyducklingcompany.com

All of these materials are offered as editable files via THL website. If you have any problems, then do let us know.

HOW TO USE YOUR PUBLICITY MATERIALS

It might seem obvious to make the following comments about how best to use the various items in THL media pack, but experience has taught us that stating the obvious is sometimes a very good idea.

POSTERS

Do put these in a prominent place. In my experience I don't think that many people will attend a course because they have seen a poster, but they can act as memory prompts if a friend has been encouraging them to think about coming along to a course.

It is important that the posters are seen by those that you want to see them. I remember visiting a church where the posters for their event for the community were being displayed inside the church.

We have created a series of six posters at various sizes that you can edit and print.

POSTCARD INVITES

With friends inviting friends being the most effective advertising strategy, we have produced some simple but attractive postcard invites to give to those individuals that you have recruited to help you fill up the course.

If you are hosting the event for an organisation, then do leave the postcards in prominent places or give them out as you talk to others.

PVC BANNERS

With a PVC banner well positioned you can let many people know about what you are about to run; you can make a bold statement about your course in a well-populated spot.

POP-UP BANNERS

Similar to a PVC banner, when well positioned, pop-up banners can be used to inform people about what you are intending to do.

As far as the printing of these resources is concerned, this can be done either via your church printer (though some of the paper sizes will not be possible) or you can take them to a professional printer and pay for them to be printed.

WORKING WITH THE MEDIA

Consider how you can harness the radio or local newspapers to let people know about the course you will be running.

However, remember that you do not have a right to be heard and there is only so much space that can be allocated to those who want to advertise an event.

Think creatively and approach your local radio station, newspaper, or even TV station to see if they would be interested in giving you a slot to talk to people.

FRIENDS INVITING FRIENDS

As we have noted above, the most effective way of gathering a group of delegates for THL is to have some individuals who are willing to invite their friends.

Depending on who you work with, it might be helpful to spend a little time helping them identify the various networks that they are involved in to discover possible candidates to invite onto the course.

Your aim should be to equip them to deal with some of the concerns that those that they are inviting might have. However good the friendship and the level of trust, many people will be unsure of what they are being invited to and concerned that they will be made to do something that they don't want to do. Some may worry about being picked on or being put on the spot or made to look stupid. Be sensitive to all of these things so that you can work to counteract them.

BOOKS

There are two books that The Ugly Duckling Company offer as extra resources. These could be useful tools in advertising your course. You might offer them as free gifts at an event that you are hosting and possibly put a postcard invite into the book too.

We mentioned both books earlier: they are *101 Happiness Experiments* and *The 8 Secrets of Happiness*.

SOCIAL MEDIA

Social media has become a very effective way to promote an event. It is possible to direct your Facebook posts to specific age groups in particular geographical areas. For only a small cost you can have your advert about your course appearing on the Facebook wall of people living in your geographic community.

It is important that you think carefully about what you want to say. Using a video seems to draw more people in more effectively. If you decide to write a post instead, then do add an image.

You can schedule your post to run for several days.

In addition to Facebook, you can also use Twitter and a number of other social media. Why not use the banner images provided for these postings too?

WEBSITES

There is a Happiness Lab website that you can point people to. For those who want to know more about what they have been invited to and what might happen during the course, then this is a great resource to promote (www.thehappinesslab.org).

If you have your own website (or the partner organisation that you are working with has a website), then do think about using some of the web banners available in the media pack; they are designed for this purpose.

PROMO AND PREVIEW VIDEO

There are two videos available. These are both included on THL DVD.

The first is a one-minute promo that opens up the idea of THL, while the other is a 10-minute preview which is ideal for a launch event.

It could be helpful to put the one-minute promo on your website or the website of the organisation that you will be working with (or both).

'For me, one of the biggest learning moments of being on The Happiness Lab was to do with the challenge to slow down a little and appreciate what is going on around me.'

LAUNCH

OVERVIEW

Launch events are important. They can act as a shop window into the whole course. For those invited to the launch event who are thinking about attending THL, it provides an opportunity to meet other possible delegates and figure out if the people facilitating the course can be trusted.

What follows below is a list of issues to think through as you plan your event.

- What is the best time to hold this event?
- Where should you host this event?
- What is the agenda for the event?

- How do you make the event relaxed, friendly and welcoming?
- What is your purpose? (show people the preview video and offer them an opportunity to attend)
- How do people sign up for the course there and then or in the weeks following?
- Is there a deadline to sign up by?
- How do potential delegates get to mingle with each other?
- Do you have sample material on display?
- Could you offer *101 Happiness Experiments* books as a gift to each attendee?

INVITING PEOPLE TO THE LAUNCH EVENT

When it comes to inviting people to the launch event, why not consider one of the following:

- Use postcard invites
- Give out *101 Happiness Experiments* with postcard inside

SUGGESTED FORMAT FOR THE EVENT

People gather for launch event, to include refreshments or possibly a meal.

Welcome given

People eat

Introduction is made about THL and an invitation is given to join the next course (show video)

People eat more

Event ends

SESS
OUTC

SESSION OUTLINES

As noted in the Format section below, each course context or location may need a different format.

It is important that you give people an opportunity to connect socially during that week's get-together. You might want to offer a meal before the event and coffee halfway through (or at the end of) the session.

For each session you will need a screen, a DVD player and speakers.

SESSION TEMPLATE

Welcome

Recap: Look at how people have got on with their exercises over the last week (this will not be used during Week 1)

Introduction to that week's session

Video: Show relevant video episode

Discussion (questions are in the session plans that follow and in the Delegate's Guide)

Happiness experiments: Look at the options for next week

Reflection
- What did you enjoy?
- What have you learned?
- What will you take away with you?

Final questions or instructions

SESSION 1: FOCUSSING ON GRATITUDE & SAVOURING

SESSION AIMS

The goal of this session is to learn the practice of savouring—what it is and its effects—and to begin to count our blessings by saying "thank you".

WELCOME TO THL

Hello everyone. My name is (insert here) and on behalf of (insert here) I want to welcome you to The Happiness Lab.

We are delighted to have you on THL and do hope that it is a meaningful experience for each one of you.

We have obtained a number of resources that we want to give you that will aid you as you travel through the course. The purpose of these resources is to help you get the best out of each session.

HAND OUT RESOURCES

We have a Delegate's Guide for each of you. As you will see from flicking through the guide, there are a number of different items that will help you engage with each week's topic. Feel free to treat the book as if it is your own. If you decide not to use it, that is of course fine.

Tips to offer for using the Delegate's Guide

- Fill in as much or as little of the guide as you want to.
- Bring this workbook with you to each of the sessions.
- Feel free to write all over the guide, marking with an "x" the bits you disagree with, a "v" the bits you do agree with and a "?" the bits you are unsure of.
- Use the guide to think back over the questions you looked at in the last session.
- Use the guide to think about the questions you will consider in the next session.
- Use the guide to go more deeply into the topic of each session.

OUTLINE COURSE

The Happiness Lab is made up of six sessions. During this time we will be exploring the following themes:

Session 1: Focussing on Gratitude & Savouring

Session 2: Practising Acts of Kindness

Session 3: Learning to Forgive

Session 4: Investing in Friends & Family

Session 5: Looking After Your Body & Soul

Session 6: Developing Coping Strategies

INTRODUCING PEOPLE TO EACH OTHER

One of the joys of life and of being on THL is the opportunity of doing the course with others. Some of you might know each other already, but there might be some who are new to the group and so for a few minutes we would like you to move around the room and say hello to different people.

GROUND RULES

It is best that the group identifies and agrees on its own ground rules. To help you encourage the group to think about what might work for them, we have listed below some examples:

- Mobile phones should be turned off.
- Everyone aim for punctuality where possible.
- Be willing to listen to others.
- Disagree politely with no personal attacks on other delegates.
- Commit to learn and engage.
- Intend to have as good a time as possible together.

INTRODUCTION TO THIS WEEK'S SESSION

In this week's session we are going to explore the topics of gratitude and savouring.

For those of you who are curious as to why we have put these two disciplines together, the reason is simple: there is a clear connection between savouring life's joys and saying "thank you" for them or "counting your blessings". It is a natural step from one to the next.

VIDEO

Episode 1: Focussing on Gratitude & Savouring

SOMETHING TO PONDER

We are keen that in each session there is an opportunity to talk about the video and hear what you think about what you have seen and also hear any questions that you might have about the topic.

(There is no need to do these questions in order.)

1. Does anyone have a question or comment that they would like to make about the video or on the topic we are looking at today?

2. What can you be thankful for today?

3. How do you spot the good things that happen in your life?

4. How do you become an ungrateful person?

5. How do you cultivate a more grateful heart?

6. Who should we be grateful to: only ourselves, the actions of others, or a divine power?

7. What does savouring mean to you?

8. What helps you savour an experience?

9. What is your top tip for slowing down to savour an experience?

10. What hinders you from savouring?

11. Why does personal loss or tragedy make some people more grateful?

12. How does savouring make you happier?

13. Who is the most miserable person you know?

14. What piece of music do you find you get lost in?

15. Describe a precious memory or the most precious gift you have ever been given.

16. Is savouring about the journey, the destination, or both? Why?

HAPPINESS EXPERIMENTS

THL is not only the place to think about what makes us happier, but also a place to experiment with different exercises that we can build into our lives to raise our happiness level.

In each chapter of THL you will find a number of exercises you can try. In addition, there is also an accompanying book entitled *101 Happiness Experiments*. This is available on iBooks/ Kindle and also as a physical book via THL website. You will also find some happiness exercises on THL website.

Keep a gratitude journal

This encourages a routine of reflection and acknowledgment of the good things that have happened recently. It also acts as a memory bank for when good experiences are less frequent.

There is no need to go through all of the following exercises. You could pick three and briefly outline them.

Write a gratitude letter

There is enormous joy to be had in expressing your thanks for something good somebody has done—however trivial it may seem.

Make a gratitude visit

Identified as one of the most powerful happiness boosters, visit someone who has been good to you in some way and say thank you.

Say "thank you" more

These are two of the most powerful words we can say to someone. Make it a habit by going through each day expressing your gratitude.

Thank-you meal

Plan a meal with those who have been kind to you so that you can thank them for their kindness.

Celebrate special days

There are certain days that we should celebrate. They are days to look forward to and prepare for, that create good memories we can dine on for weeks, if not years, to come. Identify them, celebrate them.

Share the experience with others

There is enormous joy in reminiscing with others who have been involved in an adventure, or in simply sharing your first-hand experience of something with friends.

REFLECTION

Before we bring this session to a close, I want to encourage everyone to take a few moments to sit quietly and think about the session.

As you reflect, I would encourage you to ask yourself the following three questions:

1. What did you enjoy?
2. What have you learned?
3. What will you take away with you?

CLOSING STATEMENTS, FINAL QUESTIONS, OR INSTRUCTIONS

We hope you have enjoyed the first "official" session of THL.

We look forward to seeing you next week.

If you have any questions, then do talk to one of the leaders before you leave.

Read *The 8 Secrets of Happiness* chapter (either chapter 1 if delegates want to reflect on this week or chapter 2 if they want to prepare for next week).

SESSION 2: PRACTISING ACTS OF KINDNESS

SESSION AIMS

The purpose of this session is to understand what kindness looks like, think more deeply about how it is offered and received, and plan some acts of kindness. The session begins with a review of what exercises people have tried since the last session.

WELCOME

Hello everyone and welcome back to our second session of THL. In this session we are going to explore what it means to practise acts of kindness and how that can improve our happiness level.

RECAP ON THEME OF WEEK 1 AND THEN LEAD INTO THE EXERCISES PEOPLE TRIED

20 minutes

Last week we looked at the theme of gratitude and savouring and observed the importance of opening our eyes to the many good things that are going on around us. We realised the importance of making a conscious effort to express our gratitude for them.

As part of that, at the end of last week's session, we spent a few moments identifying the different happiness experiments that we could try over the week.

At the start of each session we want to give all of you an opportunity to reflect on your experiences from trying some of these experiments over the past week.

As you think about what you want to say, it is important to note that there is no right or wrong comment to make. We want to hear your experience and allow that to act as an encouragement and moment of instruction for everyone else.

Here are some questions for you to consider:

1. What exercises did you try?

2. Were you able to practise them every day?

3. Was any day difficult? Why do you think that was?

4. How are you feeling about these contributors to happiness now? Do they work?

5. Are you noticing a difference?

6. What have you learnt about savouring and gratitude?

So, what did people try and how did it go?

INTRODUCTION TO THIS WEEK'S SESSION

In today's session we are going to explore what kindness looks like. We are going to think about how it is offered and received and also plan some acts of kindness.

Kindness was once described as the "social miracle" as it is the mechanism by which communities can care for each other and look after each other. Kindness has the potential to change the world.

Others have called it a "miracle drug" because of all of the positive side-effects that it can produce in the lives of those who practise it.

For centuries kindness has been regarded as a noble characteristic. It is listed in the seven virtues as a direct opposite to greed.

VIDEO
Episode 2: Practising Acts of Kindness

SOMETHING TO PONDER

We are keen that in each session there is an opportunity to talk about the video, what you think about what you have seen, and any questions that you might have about the topic.

(There is no need to do these questions in order.)

1. Does anyone have a question or comment that they would like to make about the video or on the topic we are looking at today?

2. Why are people kind?

3. Why does seeing someone being kind or experiencing kindness have such an awe-inspiring impact?

4. How does being kind make you happier?

5. How can you become a kinder person?

6. In what practical ways can we be kind to others?

7. What stops people from being kind?

8. Do you agree that we need an epidemic of kindness in the home? Why?

9. What are your top tips for showing kindness in the home?

10. Should you only be kind to people that you know?

11. Why do some people find it difficult to accept the kindness of others?

12. Who is the kindest person you know?

13. Describe a time when someone demonstrated kindness to you.

14. What does it mean to be kind?

15. Who was the kindest person in history?

16. Was the Good Eritrean a kind person or a stupid person?

'One of the principles that has helped me develop a kinder approach to life has been that of reflecting each evening on the day's opportunities to be kind that I have either taken up or missed. I then resolve to act better the following day.'

Lee Channer
DELEGATE

HAPPINESS EXPERIMENTS

THL is not only the place to think about what makes us happier, but also the place to experiment with different exercises that we can build into our lives to raise our happiness level.

In each chapter of THL you will find a number of exercises you can try. In addition, there is also an accompanying book entitled *101 Happiness Experiments*. This is available on iBooks/Kindle and also as a physical book via THL website. You will also find some happiness exercises on THL website.

Smile

Sadly, in today's society you have to be careful about who you smile at, when you smile, and how big your smile is, but all that aside, smile!

Words

Words have power. Take time to speak kind, positive, life-giving words to those around you.

Listen

Many people today feel incredibly lonely. Schedule an opportunity to catch up with and listen to a family member or close friend.

Help

From time to time we all need a helping hand: someone who cuts the grass, or paints the fence, or does our shopping for us. There are occasions when opening the door for someone or offering a neighbour a lift can make their lives that little bit easier.

Wisdom

The payoff of growing older is learning some of the lessons that life teaches. What about offering some time to help at your local school or youth group and share your wisdom with others? You might be surprised by the fact that you may even learn one or two things yourself.

Surprise

Break in to the mundane life that many people live and surprise them with your presence, a gift (some baking, perhaps?), or good news.

There is no need to go through all of the following exercises. You could pick three and briefly outline them.

REFLECTION

Before we bring this session to a close, I want to encourage everyone to take a few moments to sit quietly and think about the session.

As you reflect, I would encourage you to ask yourself the following three questions:

1. What did you enjoy?
2. What have you learned?
3. What will you take away with you?

CLOSING STATEMENTS, FINAL QUESTIONS, OR INSTRUCTIONS

We hope you have enjoyed the second session of THL.

We look forward to seeing you next week.

If you have any questions, then do talk to a leader before you leave.

Read *The 8 Secrets of Happiness* chapter (either chapter 2 if delegates want to reflect on this week or chapter 5 if they want to prepare for next week).

SESSION 3: LEARNING TO FORGIVE

SESSION AIMS

The goal of this session is to define forgiveness and its boundaries, to understand some of the skills needed to develop it, and to begin to think about how to practise it personally. At the start of the session we will also explore how people got on with their exercises over the last week.

WELCOME

Hello everyone and welcome back to our third session of THL. In this session we are going to explore the topic of forgiveness and how leaning to forgive can improve our happiness level.

RECAP ON THEMES OF WEEKS 1 AND 2 AND THEN LEAD INTO THE EXERCISES PEOPLE TRIED

20 minutes

Over the last two weeks we have looked at the themes of

- Gratitude and savouring and observed the importance of opening our eyes to the many good things that are going on around us. We realised the importance of making a conscious effort to express our gratitude for them.

- Practising acts of kindness and acknowledging that it is the social miracle that we can all make happen.

As we noted last week, kindness is the quality of being friendly, generous and considerate. A noble characteristic, it has the potential to make us and the people we are kind to happier.

As you may recall, at the end of last week's session we spent a few moments identifying the different happiness experiments that we could try over the week.

At the start of each session we want to give all of you an opportunity to reflect on your experiences from trying some of these experiments.

As you think about what you want to say, it is important to note that there is no right or wrong comment to make. We want to hear your experience and allow that to act as an encouragement and moment of instruction for everyone else.

Here are some questions for you to consider as you share your experiences over the last week:

1. Were there any successes? What caused the success? Were there any "excellent failures"? (A good failure is when something doesn't go to plan but we learn a lot and are not put off. Instead, we endeavour to do better next time.)

2. Did you notice a connection between acting kindly and happiness?

3. What have you learnt about acting kindly?

4. How have you got on with savouring and gratitude? Is anyone still developing these practices?

So, what did people try and how did it go?

INTRODUCTION TO THIS WEEK'S SESSION

Today's topic is probably the deepest and most difficult subject that we will deal with on THL.

For many people the topic of forgiveness is not on their list of happiness-increasing activities. What we are going to do in this session is aim to define forgiveness and its boundaries, to understand some of the skills needed to develop it, and to begin to think about how to practise it personally.

I want to re-iterate that you only need to say or disclose what you want to.

VIDEO

Episode 3: Learning to Forgive

SOMETHING TO PONDER

We are keen that in each session there is an opportunity to talk about the video, what you think about what you have seen, and any questions that you might have about the topic.

(There is no need to do these questions in order.)

1. Does anyone have a question or comment that they would like to make about the video or on the topic we are looking at today?

2. What is your definition of forgiveness?

3. What words do you associate with the word forgiveness?

4. Should you forgive someone again and again?

5. Is there anything that should never be forgiven?

6. Have you ever taken revenge on someone who has hurt you?

7. Is there someone you have never forgiven?

8. What do you do when someone won't forgive you?

9. Why is it difficult to forgive?

10. What are some of the steps to forgiving someone?

11. How can you develop your forgiveness muscles?

12. Why do spiritual people find it easier to forgive people than those who are not spiritual?

13. Is forgiveness a good thing?

14. What is the most inspiring story you know about forgiveness?

15. Do you need to be forgiven?

16. What is the relationship between justice, mercy, and forgiveness?

HAPPINESS EXPERIMENTS

THL is not only the place to think about what makes us happier, but also experiment with different exercises we can build into our lives to raise our happiness level.

In each chapter of THL you will find a number of exercises you can try. In addition, there is also an accompanying book entitled *101 Happiness Experiments*. This is available on iBooks/Kindle and also as a physical book via THL website. You will also find some happiness exercises on THL website.

There is no need to go through all of the following exercises. You could pick three and briefly outline them.

Read the stories of others who have forgiven

Read a bestselling book that details the story of someone journeying to offer forgiveness to someone who caused them harm. If there is no book that grabs your attention, then see what films are currently showing at the cinema.

Write a letter of forgiveness

Take time to write a letter to the person who wronged you. Express your pain and the consequences of their actions. Then express your forgiveness for their action(s). There is no need to actually send the letter.

Appreciate being forgiven

No one is perfect, so in all probability there will be someone in your past that you have intentionally hurt. Imagine how they must have felt by your actions and the shock you caused by hurting them. Hopefully they would have decided to forgive you. If so, consider the journey they must have travelled on to the place of reconciliation.

Imagine forgiveness

Spend some time mulling over what it would be like to forgive the person who did you wrong. Explore your negative feelings, consider the pain they caused, try and understand why they acted as they did, and mull over what steps you need to take to offer forgiveness.

Seek forgiveness of others

Is there anyone that you need forgiveness from? If appropriate, consider taking the time to either write them a letter or go to see them; let them know what you did and ask for their forgiveness.

Talking to those who have expressed forgiveness

Spend some time with someone who has expressed forgiveness to a person who has hurt them. Listen to them as they express their pain and journey to offering forgiveness.

REFLECTION

Before we bring this session to a close, I want to encourage everyone to take a few moments to sit quietly and think about the session.

As you reflect, I would encourage you to ask yourself the following three questions:

1. What did you enjoy?
2. What have you learned?
3. What will you take away with you?

CLOSING STATEMENTS, FINAL QUESTIONS, OR INSTRUCTIONS

We hope you have enjoyed the third session of THL.

We look forward to seeing you next week.

If you have any questions, then do talk to a leader before you leave.

Read *The 8 Secrets of Happiness* chapter (either chapter 5 if delegates want to reflect on this week or chapter 6 if they want to prepare for next week).

SESSION 4: INVESTING IN FRIENDS & FAMILY

SESSION AIMS

The purpose of this session is to understand and act on the fundamental importance of relationships, what makes for good relationships, and what might prevent them. There is also an opportunity to reflect on how delegates are finding the happiness exercises.

WELCOME

Hello everyone and welcome back to our fourth session of THL. In this session we are going to explore what it means to invest in our friends and family and how that can improve our happiness level.

RECAP ON THEMES OF WEEK 1, 2, AND 3 AND THEN LEAD INTO THE EXERCISES PEOPLE TRIED

20 minutes

Over the last three weeks we have looked at the themes of
- Gratitude and savouring and observed the importance of opening our eyes to the many good things that are going on around us. We realised the importance of making a conscious effort to express our gratitude for them.

- Practising acts of kindness and acknowledging that it is the social miracle that we can all make happen. It is about considering others as we also look after ourselves.

- Learning to forgive.

No one can make you forgive someone. But as we learned in the last session, there is a release that comes when we journey to the painful place of letting go.

In addition to defining what forgiveness is and its boundaries, we also looked at some of the skills needed to develop it.

As you may recall at the end of last week's session, we spent a few moments identifying the different happiness experiments that we could try over the week.

At the start of each session we want to give all of you an opportunity to reflect on your experiences from trying some of these experiments.

As you think about what you want to say, it is important to note that there is no right or wrong comment to make. We want to hear your experience and allow that to act as an encouragement and moment of instruction for everyone else.

How have you got on maintaining the other disciplines?

So, what did people try and how did it go?

INTRODUCTION TO THIS WEEK'S SESSION

This week we are going to explore the importance of investing time and energy in friends and family.

When it comes to increasing your happiness level, scientists tell us that meaningful relationships are among the most important. Relationships give us a bigger boost than having a better job, being healthy, or having more money.

This idea that relationships are the key is not a new idea. Aristotle once said, "without friendship, no happiness is possible".

VIDEO

Episode 4: Investing in Friends & Family

SOMETHING TO PONDER

We are keen that in each session there is an opportunity to talk about the video, what you think about what you have seen, and any questions that you might have about the topic.

(There is no need to do these questions in order.)

1. Does anyone have a question or comment that they would like to make about the video or on the topic we are looking at today?

2. Is self-reliance good for you?

3. Why are relationships good for you?

4. What are the ingredients of healthy and unhealthy relationships?

5. What are some of your top tips for deepening an existing relationship?

6. Is conflict in a relationship always a bad thing?

7. How do you manage conflict with your friends?

8. Describe a special moment in one of your relationships.

9. What advice would you give to someone who wanted to make new friends?

10. Why are so many people lonely today?

11. Which of your relationships are affected first when life gets busy?

12. How good are you at saying "no" to the wishes and demands on your time that others make?

13. Identify your key relationships.

14. How important is it to be known by another person?

15. Why do so many people keep a pet?

16. Describe what a good listener is like.

HAPPINESS EXPERIMENTS

THL is not only the place to think about what makes us happier, but also experiment with different exercises we can build into our lives to raise our happiness level.

In each chapter of THL you will find a number of exercises you can try. In addition, there is also an accompanying book entitled *101*

Happiness Experiments. This is available on iBooks/Kindle and also as a physical book via THL website. You will also find some happiness exercises on THL website.

Cheer each other on

Achievements become sweeter when they are shared with others. When something good happens to a friend, or when they accomplish something (big or small), make a big deal out of it. If someone close to you is rising to a challenge, cheer them on; if they are finding the going quite tough, then shout for them as loud as you can.

There is no need to go through all of the following exercises. You could pick three and briefly outline them.

Make time

Relationships blossom when they are watered with time. Often, making time to invest in friendships is about choices in how you spend your time. Research indicates that choosing to spend time with friends raises our levels of happiness.

Appreciate

Everybody is a masterpiece being prepared for the big reveal. Take time to appreciate that which is good about those close to you.

Hug

There are some for whom a hug is awkward—in some circumstances even inappropriate—but where it is possible and welcome, take time to hug your friends when you get together and when you say goodbye.

Forgive

Everyone gets it wrong at some point. There are moments when the best and most noble thing to do is to forgive and move on. This isn't saying that we should always forgive. If someone hurts you, forgiving them does not mean that you just let them hurt you again.

Reminisce

One of the great joys of life is being able to walk down memory lane with some close friends and tell the story again. Plan time with some of your oldest friends to do just that.

REFLECTION

Before we bring this session to a close, I want to encourage everyone to take a few moments to sit quietly and think about the session.

As you reflect, I would encourage you to ask yourself the following three questions:

1. What did you enjoy?
2. What have you learned?
3. What will you take away with you?

CLOSING STATEMENTS, FINAL QUESTIONS, OR INSTRUCTIONS

We hope you have enjoyed the fourth session of THL.

We look forward to seeing you next week.

If you have any questions, then do talk to someone before you leave.

Read *The 8 Secrets of Happiness* chapter (either chapter 6 if delegates want to reflect on this week or chapter 7 if they want to prepare for next week).

SESSION 5: LOOKING AFTER YOUR BODY & SOUL

SESSION AIMS

The purpose of this session is to understand ourselves as whole beings (body, mind, soul, spirit), describe the influences upon us and attend to taking responsibility for our bodies and souls. There is also an opportunity to reflect on how delegates are getting on with the happiness exercises.

WELCOME

Hello everyone and welcome back to our fifth session of THL. In this session we are going to explore what it means to take care of your body and soul, and how that can improve our happiness level.

RECAP ON THEMES OF WEEKS 1, 2, 3, AND 4 AND THEN LEAD INTO THE EXERCISES PEOPLE TRIED

20 minutes

Over the last four weeks we have looked at the themes of

- Gratitude and savouring and observed the importance of opening our eyes to the many good things that are going on around us. We realised the importance of making a conscious effort to express our gratitude for them.

- Practising acts of kindness and acknowledging that it is the social miracle that we can all make happen.

- Learning to forgive and the challenges and release that the process can bring.

- Investing in friends and family.

Good relationships are crucial to our happiness. For many of us they are a source of support and joy. What is important it that we make every effort to care and deepen them.

As you may recall at the end of last week's session, we spent a few moments identifying the different happiness experiments that we could try over the week.

At the start of each session we want to give all of you an opportunity to reflect on your experiences from trying some of these experiments.

As you think about what you want to say, it is important to note that there is no right or wrong comment to make. We want to hear your experience and allow that to act as an encouragement and moment of instruction for everyone else.

So, what did people try and how did it go?

INTRODUCTION TO THIS WEEK'S SESSION

When it comes to caring for yourself, most people acknowledge that we need to look after our mind, body, and soul.

Although there is some ambiguity as to what we mean by the terms "soul" or "spiritual", there is a general acceptance that they refer to an inner aspect of our being that gives definition to who we are.

Ideas about how to look after your body, and indeed mind, are well documented: watch what you eat and drink; work on getting a good night's sleep; do an appropriate amount of exercise; and do puzzles and games that get your mind working.

But how do we look after our soul? Admittedly, as whole beings, to look after our mind and body is to look after our soul. If we are in good shape physically, hopefully we will feel better about who we are.

What we are going to do in this session is explore how we better look after our body and soul.

VIDEO

Episode 5: Looking After Your Body & Soul

SOMETHING TO PONDER

We are keen that in each session there is an opportunity to talk about the video, what you think about what you have seen, and any questions that you might have about the topic.

(There is no need to do these questions in order.)

1. Does anyone have a question or comment that they would like to make about the video or on the topic we are looking at today?

2. Do you make time to look after yourself?

3. What do you understand by the terms "body" and "soul"?

4. How do you identify the positive and negative voices in your life?

5. What positive choices are you making to ensure that you look after yourself physically?

6. What advice would you give to someone who wanted to develop their spiritual life?

7. How do you know when your life is out of balance, and how do you rectify this?

8. Are there certain ways that you can switch off and relax?

9. What is your top tip for a good night's sleep?

10. Do you have any rituals that keep you well?

11. How do you manage your digital life?

12. Is there a place you go to find peace and quiet?

13. If laughter is the best medicine, how do we laugh more?

14. Do you pray?

15. What one thing could you stop or start to look after yourself better?

16. Why do you think looking after your body and soul will make you happier?

'MOVING TO A PLACE OF FORGIVENESS IS LIKE NO LONGER CARRYING THE BAGGAGE OF ANGER, RAGE AND BITTERNESS.'

DELEGATE PENNY KAVALARES

HAPPINESS EXPERIMENTS

Look at the options for next week.

The Happiness Lab is not only the place to think about what makes us happier, but also experiment with different exercises we can build into our lives to raise our happiness level.

In each chapter of THL you will find a number of exercises you can try. In addition, there is also an accompanying book entitled *101 Happiness Experiments*. This is available on iBooks/Kindle and also as a physical book via THL website. You will also find some happiness exercises on THL website.

Find a soul friend

Walking through life in the company of a friend makes sacred the path you travel. If you have someone in your life like this, then take time to reconnect; if not, then consider how you could go about finding and nurturing such a friendship.

There is no need to go through all of the following exercises. You could pick three and briefly outline them.

Celebration

Take time to celebrate life and the success of others.

Sacred place

It is good to have a place you can go to find peace and quiet: a sacred place where it is easier to realise that you are not alone on this planet, that there is a hand that guides your life, and that there is hope for tomorrow. Take a few moments this week to visit that place.

Laughter

It is good to laugh. Watch a funny programme on TV, visit a comedy club, go and see a comedian, or read a book of jokes.

Hospitality

We meet something of the spiritual in the lives of others. Sharing a meal with friends or acquaintances will allow you to explore each other's stories.

Service

Often in the expressing of kindness to others we encounter something of the divine. Look for opportunities where you can help someone else.

Filtering voices

From when we wake up to the moment that we go to sleep there are people communicating to us. Whether it's the DJ on the radio, the lyricist of the song you are humming or the commercials on TV, everyone has a message. Caring for your soul is about operating a filter that ensures that you only allow in that which you decide.

REFLECTION

Before we bring this session to a close, I want to encourage everyone to take a few moments to sit quietly and think about the session.

As you reflect, I would encourage you to ask yourself the following three questions:

1. What did you enjoy?
2. What have you learned?
3. What will you take away with you?

CLOSING STATEMENTS, FINAL QUESTIONS, OR INSTRUCTIONS

We hope you have enjoyed the fifth session of THL.

We look forward to seeing you next week.

If you have any questions, then do talk to someone before you leave.

Read *The 8 Secrets of Happiness* chapter (either chapter 7 if delegates want to reflect on this week or chapter 8 if they want to prepare for next week).

FACILITATOR'S NOTES

SESSION 6: DEVELOPING COPING STRATEGIES

SESSION AIMS

The purpose of this session is to explore coping strategies for when life is difficult, consider how the happiness exercises worked out over the last week, to review the whole course, and end well.

WELCOME

Hello everyone and welcome back to our final session of THL. In this session, we are going to explore what it means to develop coping strategies and how that can improve our happiness level.

RECAP ON THEMES OF WEEKS 1, 2, 3, 4, AND 5 AND THEN LEAD INTO THE EXERCISES PEOPLE TRIED

20 minutes

Remember to encourage delegates to fill out the online Happiness Lab survey, which can be found at: www.thehappinesslab.org

Over the last five weeks we have looked at the themes of

- Gratitude and savouring and observed the importance of opening our eyes to the many good things that are going on around us. We realised the importance of making a conscious effort to express our gratitude for them.

- Practising acts of kindness and acknowledging that it is the social miracle that we can all make happen.

- Learning to forgive and the challenges and release that the process can bring.

- Investing in friends and family and the joy and strength that brings.

- Looking after your body and soul.

There might be some ambiguity when it comes to understanding what we mean by soul, but there is no doubt that there is an incredible amount of interest in the subject.

As part of our previous session we spent some time thinking about what it means to care for your soul.

As you may recall at the end of last week's session, we spent a few moments identifying the different happiness experiments that we could try over the week.

At the start of each session we want to give all of you an opportunity to reflect on your experiences from trying some of these experiments.

As you think about what you want to say, it is important to note that there is no right or wrong comment to make. We want to hear your experience and allow that to act as an encouragement and moment of instruction for everyone else.

So, what did people try and how did it go?

INTRODUCTION TO THIS WEEK'S SESSION

As M. Scott Peck noted in his book *The Road Less Travelled*, life is difficult. At some point or another almost everyone goes through suffering, pain, or damaging circumstances that they would rather avoid.

For some people, life can seem like one continuous assault course. But how do you cope when life does not go as you hope or plan for?

The purpose of THL is to explore ways of becoming a happier person. To achieve that goal we have to find strategies for managing the times when life is tough. It might be too optimistic to think that we can go through difficult times "singing and dancing", but could there be a way of accepting and enduring what is going on that will not only bring us through, but also help us grow—perhaps even give us a couple of good days?

There is no one-size-fits-all when it comes to using coping strategies to deal with the sad times that life can create. What is important is to figure out what works for you—and excel at it.

VIDEO

Episode 6: Developing Coping Strategies

SOMETHING TO PONDER

We are keen that in each session there is an opportunity to talk about the video, what you think about what you have seen, and any questions that you might have about the topic.

(There is no need to do these questions in order.)

1. Does anyone have a question or comment that they would like to make about the video or on the topic we are looking at today?

2. How easy do you find it to get back up after you have been knocked down?

3. What are some of your coping mechanisms for when life is tough?

4. How have your friends helped you during some of life's difficulties?

5. Who can you turn to for help and advice when life gets tough?

6. How easy is it to accept and endure the tough stuff that happens to you?

7. Is it possible to be happy during tough times?

8. Why does the world seem to be a broken place?

9. Do you see problems as a setback, a challenge, or an opportunity?

10. Is it important how you think about why life is tough?

11. Where do you go in yourself to find strength?

12. Why do people pray during tough times?

13. What are some of the ways that we can help others when they are going through a tough time?

14. Who is the bravest person you know?

15. What coping strategies do you have that are unhealthy?

16. What is the worst thing that has ever happened to you, and how did you deal with it?

HAPPINESS EXPERIMENTS

THL is not only the place to think about what makes us happier, but also experiment with different exercises we can build into our lives to raise our happiness level.

In each chapter of THL you will find a number of exercises you can try. In addition, there is also an accompanying book entitled *101 Happiness Experiments*. This is available on iBooks/Kindle and also as a physical book via THL website. You will also find some happiness exercises on THL website.

Store up positive thoughts

As you go through life, store up for yourself positive experiences and thoughts so that when life is difficult you can draw on the positivity you have banked.

Call on friends

When life is tough, there is sometimes nothing better than a shoulder to cry on or someone with whom you can talk through your issues. If life is difficult right now, why not schedule some time with a close friend.

Take time out

Being able to get away from what is going on in your life is a great coping mechanism. It might not be possible to take a two-week holiday, but even a ten-minute walk can help re-calibrate you.

Get yourself ready

If you know in advance that life is going to get a little difficult, think through what you can do to move through that period as well as possible.

Pray

People who pray often deal with difficulty easier than those who don't. It is helpful because you don't feel alone as you go through whatever it is that is troubling you, and it enables you to step outside your immediate situation.

There is no need to go through all of the following exercises. You could pick three and briefly describe them. If there is one that has worked for you, highlight it and tell your story.

CONCLUDING THE COURSE

We hope you have benefited from being a delegate on THL.

As we draw this session together and as the course comes to an end, I thought it would be useful for us to take a few moments to reflect on our experience over the last six weeks and determine how we might move forward.

I want to encourage everyone to take a few moments to sit quietly and think about this session.

As you reflect, I would encourage you to ask yourself the following three questions:

1. What did you enjoy about the course?
2. What have you learned on the course?
3. What will you take away with you from the course?

LETTERS

I want to encourage you to identify three things that you are going to do as a result of being on this course. Once you have done that, I want you to take one of these envelopes and card, address it to yourself, write the three resolutions on the card, and put it in the envelope. We will post this letter to you in six weeks' time. The reason that it will be in six weeks is that according to psychologists, it takes 42 days or six weeks for new habits to be built in to someone's life.

Thank you for being a part of The Happiness Lab.

SURVEY

Before people leave, encourage them to fill in THL survey online.

'I think I have a new depth to how I live my life: far more than the shallowness of just running the treadmill.'

Alison Clarke

DELEGATE

DELEGATES

W HO ARE WE TRYING TO CONNECT WITH?

THL is designed for those who want to go on a journey—one might say an adventure—to discover what exactly it means to be happy.

Ideally, participants should be willing to make a six-week commitment to the group. Over that time they will be encouraged by you and the material to think about the ideas they are encountering and to have a go at some of the exercises.

From experience, running THL attracts a number of people who are dealing with depression. Do encourage them to seek professional medical help if this is the case.

WHO ARE YOUR POTENTIAL DELEGATES?

Most people attend an event or course because one of their friends has done the course or would like to have a go at it themselves and is keen to have someone go along with them.

Some of the courses you run will have a ready-made group (place of work) or marketing network (gym). In those contexts where you are gathering your own crowd, then it is noted that the best way to bring people together for a course is to encourage individuals to invite their friends.

We address how people can invite their friends along in the section on marketing.

As you will notice from the marketing materials available, there is a postcard invite that can be used. The postcard is a useful tag to stimulate a conversation and act as a reminder.

REFUSALS AND DROPOUTS

It is obviously sad if someone refuses to join the course having heard about it, or drops out part-way through. However, this is an accepted part of putting on any event like this. Do not take "no-shows" as a personal failure. Life is complicated sometimes.

When engaging with those who have missed one or two sessions, it is important to give them permission to stop coming along if life is just too much for them at that moment. If you sense that they just need extra encouragement, then be sure to offer it.

If someone did connect with the group but then stopped attending, why not try and stay in touch with them. If appropriate, give them an opportunity to engage with the next course that you run.

STAYING IN TOUCH

When we ran our trial course in Lydney in Gloucestershire, each week two of the delegates contacted each other to encourage the other to keep attending. We are not aware that they knew each other before the course began, but they seemed to strike up an instant connection and so would be sure to let the other person know that they would be there the following week.

We would encourage you to tell that story to your group and inspire them to think about the other members of the group, encouraging each other to be there at each session. The group is richer and people receive far more when they travel with the same people over the six weeks.

If time permits and your team is large enough, why not make sure that all of the delegates are contacted every week.

DISCUSSION GROUP

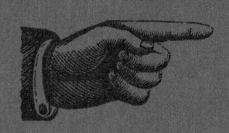

INTRODUCTION

Discussion groups are important. In facilitating a good discussion group you are giving the delegates an opportunity to think through what they have heard, engage with the opinions of others, and reflect on the impact of that session on them.

BE FRIENDLY

Do make an effort to be friendly to everyone. As the course unfolds you will gravitate to some more than others, but it is important to give all present a warm welcome.

ASK GOOD QUESTIONS

The questions offered in the Delegate's Guide are a starting place. Do not feel that you have to ask these questions or tackle them in the order they are presented.

If at all possible, take time before the session to work through the questions asked and consider how you would answer them.

An alternative way to start each session could be to ask delegates if they had any questions following what they have seen on the video.

When it comes to stimulating good conversations, we might ask:

- a question to clarify what is being said

- a question to help someone examine what they are saying

- a question to help someone take a next step in their understanding

- a question in response to another question

- a supplementary question to clarify an initial question

- a question to draw others into the discussion

- a question to defuse a tense situation.

The idea is not to try and trip people up; rather, we are asking questions that will open up the best discussion and moment of learning.

LISTEN WELL

We all know that the key to good communication is the ability to listen. The sentiment slips off the tongue easily and is nearly always heard with nodding acknowledgment, but that is a long way from actually being modelled and being a core competency in a group.

Communication experts inform us that people are more likely to listen to us if we first listen to them, but that is not why we listen. Listening to someone is attributing to them the worth that they have.

True listening builds relationship and also develops empathy.

Good listening includes:

- listening with your ears – 10 per cent from the words and 40 per cent from the tone

- listening with your eyes – most of what someone communicates is non-verbal, which is where our eyes help us: body language, facial expression, posture and gestures

- listening with your heart – listening to the emotion being communicated: feeling something of what they are saying

- listening with our mouths – clarifying questions, to ensure we have heard correctly

- listening with our spirit – we are all spiritual beings on a journey of discovery.

Listening is not waiting for them to draw breath so you can chip in. Rather, it is being fully engaged and sharing fully in the act of communication.

JOURNEY TOGETHER

No one knows it all; we are all life-long learners. As a group of individuals, everyone has something worth sharing. The skill of the group leader is to provide a space and atmosphere where everyone can speak if they want to and no one is forced to speak if they don't.

TALK HONESTLY ABOUT YOUR EXPERIENCE

The definition of what it means to be an expert has changed. Once, your authority for being an expert was that you held more information about a particular subject than anyone else. Today, with the availability of information on the Internet and the belief that there is more to understanding a topic than just academic knowledge, people want to hear about other people's experiences.

As course facilitator, this creates an appropriate space for you to say something about your own journey. It is important that you use words and concepts that resonate with your delegates.

Added to this must be the acknowledgment that you do not know it all: that you are not perfect and that you have, and are, making mistakes along the way.

ENCOURAGE OPEN, HONEST CONVERSATION

As noted above, we want to encourage open and honest conversations. When someone says something that others do not like, ensure that no personal verbal attack follows.

That said, it is important that people are able to make challenging statements.

UNEXPECTED CONVERSATIONS

There are moments in every course when a discussion begins which almost defines the group.

Often in that one conversation it becomes obvious who they are, where they are in their journey, and what they need to think more deeply about.

Of course, there are a number of red herrings that you have to be able to spot and navigate through, but when that defining question is aired there is no need to close it down or be worried that you will not cover the rest of the material in that session.

When these questions are aired be sure to allow space, time, and silence to be part of the discussion. For some people this will be the first time that they have given expression to their thoughts, particularly in public. If you have the skill set, try to read the whole room.

HOW TO DEAL WITH SENSITIVE ISSUES

Not every thought that pops into a delegate's mind should be shared. Unfortunately, not everyone has the ability to filter what should and should not be said. As course facilitator it is your job to create a space that guards people from making comments that they might later regret.

Should something deeply precious be communicated to the group, then do think through the impact of those revelations on other group members and the vulnerability that the person making the disclosure has accepted.

This is the time to care for and guard the lives of your delegates.

It can be appropriate to have a very honest conversation about sensitive issues. What is vital is that those engaged in that discussion are cared for.

STOPPING AND SILENCE

Many of us are surrounded by noise—far too much noise. Others have lives that can only be described as busy.

With this being so, two of the greatest gifts that we can bring to the group are an opportunity to slow down a little—if not to stop—and spend time in silence.

silence

Max Ehrmann - Desiderata

GROUP SIZE

Until the course kicks off, you will have no real idea of how many people will be attending. What's more, that same uncertainty is played week in, week out as you deal with those who decide to drop out or don't show up for that particular week.

A few considerations:

- Do you have one group?

- Do you mix the groups each week?

- What would work for those on the course?

- Groups of six work well, whereas a group of more than 12 could be too big.

- Flexible approach: if it doesn't work, change it.

- Allow friends to stay together unless they request to be in different groups.

GROUND RULES

It is useful to set a few ground rules from the outset:

- Respect one another's opinions

- Listen to each other carefully

- No interrupting

- It is OK to disagree with someone's opinion

- It is OK to be silent (no picking on people)

- People are welcome to express their emotions.

PERSONALITY TYPES

Each of us is unique, yet it is possible to group your delegates into different personality types. Your group will have a mix of types.

As a result, do think through how you engage with each member of the group so as to bring out the best in them.

DIFFICULT PEOPLE

What would you define as a difficult person? Is a difficult person someone who does not speak or speaks too much? Is it someone who agrees with everything you say or completely disagrees with everything you say? Is it someone who tries to lead the group off in a different direction or asks questions that seem too shallow or too deep for where you are in your discourse?

In most—if not all—cases, a difficult person is only a matter of our perspective. With regard to dealing with such an individual in a group context there are a few tools at your disposal, but the real work is done outside the group as you develop a relationship with them. Once you have developed a relationship it is possible to manage the space that you give them during group discussions and to help them understand their impact on everyone else. This latter conversation should happen privately for it to be most effective.

ENCOURAGE USE OF THE DELEGATE'S GUIDE

The questions from last week and for next week are in each section. Encourage participants to think through what is ahead or reflect on what was discussed.

PRACTICALITIES

No two courses are identical. There might be some similarities in running a course, but more often than not each scenario will demand some flexibility and a different approach.

Below we have attempted to identify and comment on some of the key practical issues in running THL. Once you have run the course, if you can think of material that needs to be added to our list or perhaps a correction to what is there, then please do contact us and give us your thoughts and insight so that they can be shared with others.

TIMELINE

- Purchase materials and become familiar with them.

- Gather volunteers together.

- Agree on a venue, dates, numbers and format.

- Advertise the course and invite people.

- Launch event.

- Start the course.

- When the course is finished, take some time to think about how the course went.

- Three months after the end of the course, invite delegates to get together for a meal and reflect on how things are going.

- Six months after the end of the course, invite delegates to a half-day workshop going over some of the material you covered in the course.

FORMAT

The first Happiness Lab we ran lasted for two hours, from 19:15 to 21:15, on a Wednesday night. To make life easier for those attending the course we offered a free meal available from 18:30 at the venue. Halfway through a session we offered some refreshments, which also gave people an opportunity to take a comfort break. At the end of the evening, thinking that people would want to leave as quickly as possible, we did not offer an opportunity for people to stay around and chat. Despite the lack of refreshments, as the weeks went on they stayed longer and longer to talk.

None of the above is compulsory, or necessarily the best way of putting on THL. Courses work better when groups spend time together; the meal each week provided that opportunity. Refreshments at the end of the evening might also work well.

Think through what could work in your location and give it a go. One way forward would be to ask the group what would work for them.

FOOD AND REFRESHMENTS

Some groups offer a meal before each session and some offer nothing. It is a good idea, though, to offer some refreshments halfway through a session as it gives everyone an opportunity to get some space and engage with other delegates on a more informal level. Some groups would benefit from serving refreshments as people arrive or at the end of the evening.

VENUE

To run THL you will need a space where people can sit, where a DVD can be played, and where people can easily engage in conversation with each other.

As you will be showing a DVD, check how sunlight affects the room.

Throughout the course, opportunity will be given for delegates to talk about issues that are personal to them. As a result, it is important to provide a space where people feel comfortable doing that. It will be harder for people to open up if they think they can easily be overheard by those who have nothing to do with the course.

IDEAS OF WHERE TO RUN THE COURSE

Every community is different; it might not be possible or feasible to run the course in some of the venues listed below. What we are trying to suggest in putting this list together is that you think about where is the best place to host your event. Just because you have always hosted courses in a particular place does not mean that that is the best place to run THL, and neither does it mean that you should not run it where you have always provided courses.

As noted above, when listing the possible venues of running THL, there are many contexts into which it could fit.

What about a local doctor's surgery hosting a course for some of its patients or the community at large?

Try the local health club to see if they would be interested in hosting a class.

A local church could host THL for its members, those on the fringe of the church, or those in the local community.

It could be part of the courses offered at the local Life-long Learning Centre.

A family centre might run it for those who make use of their facilities.

The local pub could run it for its regulars.

An extended family could get together on a weekly basis and explore the material together.

An employer might create space to gather workers together and explore the topic of happiness together.

A university might run it as part of Freshers' Week.

TRAINING FROM UDC

As creators of THL, we are keen to equip and encourage those who run the course to do so to the best of their ability in order that delegates have as good an experience as possible.

Consequently, we offer a two-hour training event for those who decide to run the DVD-based course. Do contact the office for more information.

EQUIPMENT NEEDED

To play the DVD you need either a DVD player or a computer.

Depending on the size of the group, you will either need to show the footage on a TV or through a data projector and screen.

It is important that people are able to easily hear what is being said by the host and from those on the DVD, and so ensure that there is sufficient amplification for the size of the room.

Some people like to run courses with delegates around tables, while others prefer a more relaxed format of sitting in soft chairs.

A flip-chart could be helpful.

FREQUENCY OF SESSIONS

You know the group you are working with better than us, so the decision is yours.

Clearly there are a number of options: daily, weekly, fortnightly, monthly. You might decide to do a weekend intensive session or spread the material over a year.

To give delegates time to digest the content of each session and explore some of the practices that go with the topic they have looked at, we would suggest aiming at a weekly event. Many people are familiar with the idea of signing up for a short course run with a weekly class.

MONEY/BUDGET

SHOULD YOU CHARGE DELEGATES TO ATTEND THL?

In some circumstances you will have no input into that decision; if the course is run in partnership with a local health club, FE college, or at your doctor's surgery then that decision will often be made for you. You might decide not to ask for a facilitator's fee, but if the host organisation has a habit of charging for the courses that they put on, then it might be mandatory.

'Happiness comes from living well. You live well when you realise you are a spiritual person in a material age.'

Paul Griffiths & Martin Robinson

If the course is hosted in a location that you are in charge of, then there will be greater flexibility. There is still the issue of covering the cost of materials, any refreshments you provide, and the expense of asking someone to lead or facilitate the course; obviously how you decide to cover that cost is up to you.

In some circumstances it might be appropriate to ask for voluntary donations.

HOW MUCH DOES IT COST TO HOST THL?

When it comes to calculating the cost of running THL, the following factors should be taken into consideration:

- cost of venue use or hire

- cost of materials

- cost of refreshments served

- cost of a facilitator or course leader (if paid)

- hire of any equipment needed

- publicity costs.

SETTING UP

Last-minute preparations rarely help anyone. They might encourage focus and provide an adrenalin rush, but in the long term not only do they exhaust those involved in facilitating the course, they also increase the possibility of something being forgotten.

Admittedly, life can be demanding at times and on occasion it might be necessary to leave everything to the last minute. When that happens, do your best and don't overdose on guilt.

Depending on the number of helpers available, why not appoint someone to be your deputy and take responsibility of setting everyone up for each session?

VOLUNTEERS

You want volunteers who are willing to ensure that the delegates have as good a time as possible. Think about the people that you choose to help you facilitate the course. No one is perfect, and we are all carrying issues that we are dealing with. That said, the course is an opportunity for the volunteer to put others first.

Do consider gathering the volunteers together before the event so that they get to know each other and understand their role and also the role of others.

It is always good to express your gratitude to volunteers in front of delegates and also personally, once the course is finished.

TIMING

A session can last anything from 60 minutes to 120 minutes with refreshments.

A rough guide for a 90-minute session would be:

Recap: 20 minutes
Introduction to that session: 5 minutes
Video: 25 minutes
Discussion: 25 minutes
Exercises: 10 minutes
Conclusion: 5 minutes

QUESTIONS TO ASK YOURSELF BEFORE YOU RUN THL

- Who will attend your course?

- Where shall we host the course?

- Do we want to run the course ourselves or would we like to offer it through an agency such as University of the Third Age, or the local GP or health club? Maybe the local FE college would be interested in hosting it?

AFTER THE HAPPINESS LAB

In attending THL, delegates are signing up for a six-week course. Once the course ends then there are no official additional expectations on attendees. The course is designed to be self-standing and an end in itself.

That said, our experience from running THL is that often some, if not all, of the group will like the idea of getting together in some way after the course ends.

Listed below are a number of options you might consider.

3-MONTH MEAL

The first Happiness Lab was run from September-October. Aware that people were missing meeting together, we organised a Christmas meal as an opportunity for them to get together for an evening and catch up. Obviously, depending on when you run your course, Christmas might not be the best time to organise a three-month get together.

6-MONTH HALF-DAY

We often bumped into those who attended our first Happiness Lab and many asked if we could spend a longer period of time together to catch up on how we were all doing.

HAPPY HINTS EMAIL

Aware that some people want and require continued stimulation as they build their happiness muscles, we publish a regular happiness email full of ideas, news and encouragement. Do sign up for this email yourself and encourage those on the course to do so also.

LYDNEY STORY

Our first Happiness Lab happened in Lydney, our local town. It was a slightly artificial group, as the delegates were there to help us "road test" the material and to be filmed in the process. They are the characters that you meet in THL DVD.

We had such a good time together on the course that there was a very real sense of missing each other when the course ended. Some of us work in the same office block and so we were able to catch up a little during the week, but the general feeling of the group was that it would be good to stay in touch.

As noted above, we organised a three-month get-together meal. This was our way of saying thank you to those who tested the material for us, but also a way of us getting together and catching up as a group.

We were a small group of about 12, of which the six women decided that they would like to carry on meeting when the course ended. Discovering that we also publish a series of conversational games, they opted to get together and play Table Talk for Women. Some very real friendships are developing in that group. They are now talking about going away together for 24 hours as an evening doesn't seem to be long enough for them to eat and talk.

Again, following the prompting of the group and not wanting to impose any sense of expectation on those who attended the course, the idea of us all getting together for half a day has been proffered so that we can catch up with each other and reflect on how delegates are getting on with their happiness journals.

IDEAS ON HOW TO FOLLOW UP

As noted above, we are not asking people to commit to meeting with those who attended THL with them after the course is over.

That said, we do want to give people the opportunity to gather with others and reflect on how it has gone since the course finished and receive a fresh boost to keep practising the disciplines for themselves.

So, with that in mind you could consider one or some of the following:

- Phone each of the delegates once a month for the three months after the course is finished.

- Encourage everyone to be part of a Facebook group and to keep in touch with each other.

- Organise a Table Talk group to meet on a monthly basis.

- Send out a monthly text to all those who attended your course.

- Invite everyone to meet for a meal each month, for three months, following the end of the course.

- Arrange a half-day get-together after six months to reflect on where everyone is and how they have found the disciplines.

- Arrange an annual get-together.

50% of your happiness is linked to your DNA and 10% is determined by your environment, but 40% is alterable.

THE HAPPINESS LAB WEBSITE

- Sign up for our newsletter.
- Offer feedback as delegate or course leader.
- See what others who have already been on the course or facilitated it have to say.
- Find out information about THL, including stories of others who have run the course.
- Discover links to other material.
- Shop for additional material for those on the course.

www.thehappinesslab.org

ADDITIONAL INFORMATION

Additional information and material for the subjects covered on THL can be accessed via THL website.

This includes expert and delegate videos, additional questions, news on course development, and much, much more.

MARKETING MATERIALS

VIDEO
One-minute promo video
Ten-minute preview video

BOOKS
101 Happiness Experiments
The 8 Secrets of Happiness

PRINTED MEDIA
Postcards
Posters

SOCIAL MEDIA
Web banners
Facebook banner
Twitter banner

MISCELLANEOUS
Data slides
PVC banner
Pop-up banners

'I realised h

and that I h

outlook on fri

then I have t

greater intere

more about,

v busy I was

d a cynical

ndships. Since

ied to take a

t in, and think

ther people.'

Adam Matthews, Delegate

INFOR-
MATION

About...

THE UGLY DUCKLING COMPANY

The Ugly Duckling company is a registered charity. As a not-for-profit organisation we are committed to stimulating conversations around the big and not-so-big questions of life.

Rather than inform people how they should think, our goal is to create space so that individuals and communities can explore the big questions, articulate their thoughts and engage with the opinions of others.

RESOURCES THAT WE HAVE CREATED

Puzzling Questions is a six-week course for those who want to think through some of life's more profound questions.

> Who am I?
> What is God like?
> How can I be happy?
> What happens after I die?
> Why is there suffering in the world?
> What is the spiritual realm and how does it impact my life?

Table Talk is a conversational game. There are a variety of versions available.

> These includes games for young people, families at Christmas, the retired, friends gathering together, groups of women, and groups of men.

> Further information can be obtained from visiting www.table-talk.org

The Big Conversation is a twelve-month community programme that stimulates a conversation around what it means to flourish together and as individuals.